The Woman in Black

A ghost play

Adapted by **Stephen Mallatratt**
from the book by **Susan Hill**

Samuel French — London
New York - Toronto - Hollywood

THE WOMAN IN BLACK

First performed at the Stephen Joseph Theatre in the Round, Scarborough, on 11th December, 1987, with the following cast:

Actor	Jon Strickland
Kipps	Dominic Letts
The Woman	Lesley Meade

Directed by Robin Herford
Designed by Michael Holt

It was subsequently presented by the Lyric, Hammersmith, London, by arrangement with Peter Wilson and H. M. Tennent Ltd. on 11th January, 1989, with the following cast:

Actor	Charles Kay
Kipps	John Duttine
The Woman	Nicola Sloane

Directed by Robin Herford
Designed by Michael Holt

The production transferred to the Strand Theatre, London, on 15th February 1989; to the Playhouse, London, on 18th April, 1989 and to the Fortune Theatre, London, on 7th June 1989, with the same cast, where it ran in excess of five years with several cast changes.

CHARACTERS

Actor
Kipps
The Woman

The action takes place in a small Victorian theatre

With special thanks to Peter Lassey
and the Scarborough Innovation Centre

Adaptor's Note

Directors are unlikely to have much experience of ghost plays as there are relatively few around, so at the risk of stating the obvious I think it's worth a word or two concerning staging. I've now seen many productions of *The Woman in Black* around the world, some very effective, others less so.

The intent of the show is to frighten - so if it doesn't, it's nothing. The fear is not on a visual or visceral level, but an imaginative one. There are no gouts of blood nor any but the simplest of special effects.

Darkness is a powerful ally of terror, something glimpsed in a corner is far more frightening than if it's fully observed. Sets work best when they accommodate this - when things unknown might be in places unseen.

I have seen a production where the Woman herself was in full light for all her manifestations, and centre stage. Few things could have been less frightening. In the current London production we deny the audience a satisfying look at her until her final moment, and only then does she appear in all her terrifying despair.

The only aspect of the play that has any claim to complexity is the sound plot. There's also scope, though no obligation, for a wealth of light cues. In general, simple, straightforward staging is the most effective. For example there are one or two moments when just by raising the volume of a sound cue to an unexpected level, the audience can be shocked to screaming pitch.

There are anachronisms and geographical inconsistencies within the text. These are not mistakes, but indications of the neverland we inhabit when involved with the Woman in Black.

Stephen Mallatratt
January 1998

NOTE

Please note that the issue of a licence to perform this
play requires that any advertising or publicity material
(including programmes) must bear the following credit:

THE WOMAN IN BLACK
adapted by
STEPHEN MALLATRATT
from the book by
SUSAN HILL

Also by Stephen Mallatratt
published by Samuel French Ltd

An Englishman's Home ...

ACT I

A small Victorian theatre

The proscenium has its gilding and its cherubs, and the curtains are gathered at the sides revealing a stage that is unprepared for performance and devoid of scenery. On the stage is a clutter of cloths, boxes and furniture. This clutter will evolve according to the needs of the perform- ance — though should include a couple of chairs, a rocking chair, a high stool, a blanket and a large skip or trunk. A gauze divides the upstage area from the downstage. Beyond it, though unseen until lit, odd shapes of furniture are shrouded in cloths. The action, until stated, takes place in the downstage area and in the aisle of the theatre. A door is placed at the side of the stage. This door, which is presumably a remnant from some previous production, stands firmly closed

The House Lights remain on and working Lights come up on the stage

A middle-aged man enters. He carries a manuscript. He stands on the stage. This man, whose name is Kipps, will not be referred to as "Kipps" but as "Actor" — even though he clearly isn't one

At the back of the theatre, in amongst the seats, a young man enters. This man, who is an actor, will not be referred to as "Actor" but as "Kipps"

The House Lights remain on as the Actor on the stage begins to read from his manuscript

Actor (*reading*) It was nine-thirty on Christmas Eve. As I crossed the long entrance hall of my house, on my way from the dining-room, where we had just enjoyed the first of the happy, festive meals, towards the drawing-room and the fire around which my family were now assem- bled, I paused, and then, as I often do in the course of an evening, went to the front door, opened it and stepped outside.

Kipps (*from the body of the theatre*) This is intended to be of interest, I take it?

Actor Why, yes, of course.

Kipps They why announce it as if it were the fatstock prices?

Actor I'm afraid I don't understand.

Kipps Let us *see* this entrance hall, let us *see* this house, let us taste and smell this happy, festive meal!

Actor But that's impossible.

Kipps No, sir! Draw on your emotions, and on our imaginations.

Actor Forgive me, I am not an actor.

Kipps No. (*Pause*) Again. Try it again.

Actor (*reading*) It was nine-thirty on Christmas Eve. As I crossed the long entrance hall of my house, on my way from the dining-room, where we had just enjoyed the first of the happy, festive meals ——

Kipps You will excuse me. I know that what you read holds particular significance for you. That it is possible it will cause you some distress. But I must implore you: have sympathy for your audience.

Actor Sir?

Kipps Just now we are alone here in this theatre. These rows of empty seats are unlikely to protest as you hum and mumble through your lines. But believe me, sir — speak them thus before an audience and you'll see them one by one expire with boredom.

Pause

Actor It was nine-thirty on Christmas Eve. As I crossed the long entrance hall of my house, on my ——

Kipps *Long* entrance hall?

Actor That's right.

Kipps Why long?

Actor Because it is.

Kipps Have sympathy for your audience. Are they interested in its length?

Pause

Actor I apologize. I am clearly wasting your time. (*He puts his manuscript in his pocket and moves to leave*)

Kipps Stay where you are.

Actor This is a foolish adventure. I should never have come.

Kipps You did, however. And you have paid me for the day. I have no intention of not giving you full value.

Actor Please, I ——
Kipps No, sir. Attempt to leave and I will leap upon you and compel you to recite the Sonnets in their entirety!
Actor I ——
Kipps No! We'll make an Irving of you yet.
Actor I have no desire to be an Irving. All I wish, implore, is that this tale of mine be told. Be told and — laid to rest. God willing. So I may sleep without nightmares.
Kipps Which is why you came to me.
Actor Yes.
Kipps As one practised in these things.
Actor Yes.
Kipps As one who will impart to you the rudiments of public speaking, who will offer advice as to *expression* and *delivery*, and, above all, instill in you the *confidence* to stand up and make a go of it!
Actor Confidence?
Kipps Yes, *confidence*! Now then. Nine-thirty. Christmas Eve. Excitement. Anticipation. Crisp air. Crackling fires. Children asleep with stockings by their beds, a happy family, content, delighted, and above all — *at peace*.

Pause. The Actor summons up his energies

Actor It was nine-thirty on Christmas Eve. As I crossed the long — the — entrance hall of my house, on my way from — on my way ... (*Pause*) It was nine-thirty on Christmas Eve. (*Pause*) It was nine-thirty on Christmas Eve ——
Kipps What time was it?
Actor Nine-thirty ——
Kipps Not on Christmas Eve by any chance? Good gracious!
Actor I'm very sorry, this clearly isn't a success, I ——
Kipps You see, it doesn't come in five minutes. You think to stand up, recite your tale, and have your audience hang upon your words. As if that's all it takes. In which case, why d'you come to me for help? So that I'll say, "yes, wonderful, without a flaw"? Believe me, sir, performing is an art acquired with *tears* and *time*. I would be encouraged, sir, if every time I offered some advice you would not put up your manuscript and make to stalk out of the theatre!
Actor Advice?

Kipps Yes! *Advice!*

Actor It sounds more like reproval.

Kipps I promise you that as the day goes on it's likely to sound more so.

Actor May I just say — it is not a *performance* that I wish to give. No. I think we are at a misunderstanding in that respect. I wish to — speak it. No more. For my family, only. For those who need to know. I am not a performer — I have no pretensions to be — nor inclination — but — those terrible things that happened to me — they must — I *have* to — let them be told. For my health and reason.

Kipps You say you're not a performer.

Actor Oh truly.

Kipps In your hand is a manuscript which, on estimate, will take five hours to read. If you, as an acknowledged non-performer, should stand before an audience, however friendly, and drone at them for longer than it takes to play *King Lear*, I trust you will be unsurprised if by the end of it they're either fast asleep or at your throat.

Actor Five hours?

Kipps At least.

Actor Good heavens. (*Pause*) I'd no idea — I — five *hours*? (*Pause. He slumps into a chair*) I cannot possibly. (*Pause. At length he looks up. Addressing Kipps*) It must be told. I cannot carry the burden any longer. It *must* be *told*.

Black-out. When the Lights return, the House Lights stay off. Kipps is now on the stage, with the manuscript. Kipps reads it rather well. A bit actorish, certainly, but with enthusiasm and skill. The Actor walks to the back of the theatre to listen

Kipps (*reading*) It was nine-thirty on Christmas Eve. As I opened my front door and stepped outside I smelled at once, and with a lightening heart, that there had been a change in the weather. All the previous week we had had thin chilling rain and a mist that lay low about the house and over the countryside. My spirits have for many years been excessively affected by the weather. But now the dampness and fogs had stolen away like thieves into the night, the sky was pricked over with stars and the full moon rimmed with a halo of frost. Upstairs, three children slept with stockings tied to their bedposts. There was something in the air that night. That my peace of mind was about to be disturbed, and memories awakened that I had thought forever dead, I had, naturally, no idea. That

I should ever again renew my acquaintance with mortal dread and terror of spirit, would have seemed at that moment impossible. I took a last look at the frosty darkness, sighed contentedly, and went in, to the happy company of my family. At the far end of the room stood the tree, candlelit and bedecked, and beneath it were the presents. There were vases of white chrysanthemums, and in the centre of the room a pyramid of gilded fruit and a bowl of oranges stuck all about with cloves, their spicy scent filling the air and mingling with the wood-smoke to be the very aroma of Christmas. I became aware that I had interrupted the others in a lively conversation. "We are telling ghost stories — just the thing for Christmas Eve!" And so they were — vying with each other to tell the horridest, most spine-chilling tale. They told of dripping stone walls in uninhabited castles and of ivy-clad monastery ruins by moon-light, of locked inner rooms and secret dungeons, dank charnel houses and overgrown graveyards, of howlings and shriekings, groanings and scuttlings. This was a sport, a high-spirited and harmless game among young people, there was nothing to torment and trouble me, nothing of which I could possibly disapprove. I did not want to seem a killjoy, old, stodgy and unimaginative. I turned my head away so that none of them should see my discomfiture. "And now it's your turn." "Oh no," I said, "nothing from me." "You must know at least one ghost story, everyone knows *one*." Ah, yes, yes, indeed. All the time I had been listening to their ghoulish, lurid inventions, the one thought that had been in my mind, and the only thing I could have said was "No, no, you have none of you any idea. This is all nonsense, fantasy, it is not like this. Nothing so blood-curdling and becreepered and crude — not so ... so laughable. The truth is quite other, and altogether more terrible. "I am sorry to disappoint you," I said. "But I have no story to tell!" And went quickly from the room and from the house. I walked in a frenzy of agitation, my heart pounding, my breathing short. I had always known in my heart that the experience would never leave me, that it was woven into my very fibres. Yes, I had a story, a true story, a story of haunting and evil, fear and confusion, horror and tragedy. But it was not a story to be told around the fireside on Christmas Eve.

Pause. Kipps looks out to the Actor at the back of the theatre

And then I thought you might recite the piece from *Hamlet*.
Actor *Hamlet?*

Kipps "Some say that ever 'gainst that season comes ..."

Actor Oh yes, of course. (*A beat*) You then, for the purpose of the reading, become me?

Kipps Quite so. And you — for the purpose of the *performance* — you draw on your remembrance, to be the people that you met, those that played their parts in your story.

Actor Sir, I am not a performer.

Kipps Sir, I know.

Actor And this must *not* be entertainment. Those most horrible events will *not* be treated as amusement or diversion. I *insist*, sir!

Kipps And *I* insist, that you consider your audience. No matter how horrible, if your tale is to be heard, it must be offered in a form that is remotely palatable. You have come for advice and assistance, you must trust me. (*Pause*) From here, if you please.

The Actor climbs reluctantly on to the stage

And let us show that we mean business ...

Kipps switches off the workers, leaving them in a performance state

So your cue is "... fear and confusion, horror and tragedy. But it was not a story to be told around the fireside on Christmas Eve."

Actor (*reading from a copy of the manuscript*)
"Some say that ever 'gainst that season comes
Wherein our Saviour's birth is celebrated,
This bird of dawning singeth all night long.
And then, they say, no spirit dare stir abroad,
The nights are wholesome, then no planets strike,
No Fairy takes, nor witch hath power to charm
So hallowed and so gracious is that time."

Kipps Those lines came into my head as if from heaven, and a great peace came upon me. I recalled that the way to banish an old ghost that continues its hauntings is to exorcise it. Well, then. Mine should be exorcised. I should tell my tale. I should set it down on paper, with every care and in every detail. I would write my own ghost story, and then, that they might know and that I might be forever purged of it, relive it through the telling. I prayed a heartfelt, simple prayer for peace of mind, and for strength and steadfastness to endure while I completed the most agonizing task. The first part, the writing, I have done. Now comes the telling. I pray for God's protection on us all.

Black-out

The Actor exits

The Lights come up. It's the worker state again, though the House Lights are now down and remain so for the rest of the evening. Kipps is on stage, arranging the clutter of furniture into some order that can pass for a solicitor's office. The skip suggests a large partners' desk

The Actor enters

Good-morning!
Actor Good-morning.
Kipps I trust you slept well?
Actor Thank you, yes.
Kipps No nightmares?
Actor Not too bad, I thank you.
Kipps Ah. So we are not clear of it yet?
Actor I fear I never will be.
Kipps We'll have you playful as a lamb again, you mark my words. Did you study as I asked you?
Actor As best I can — you must excuse me, it is not my ... forte.
Kipps We'll make an Irving of you yet.
Actor (*irritably*) I have no wish to be an Irving.
Kipps No. But for the sake of our audience, let us at least try.
Actor This audience you speak of — it is to be just my family and friends? You don't intend to make a public spectacle ——
Kipps Good heavens, no. Your family, your friends. Perhaps the odd theatre manager, but ... Now then — scene: London. Interior of the offices of solicitors Bentley, Haigh, Sweetman and Bentley. And I have a little surprise for you.
Actor What's that?
Kipps Thank you, Mr Bunce! (*He clicks his fingers to the back of the theatre*)

Instantly come the sound effects of a London Street: cars, horses, shouts

*from street vendors, etc. The Actor is momentarily amazed. He listens for
a while, then ...*

Actor Recorded sound!
Kipps Precisely. A remarkable invention, is it not?
Actor Extraordinarily true to life! I could swear I was in a London street,
attempting to negotiate the thundering traffic!
Kipps And so, Mr Kipps, will our audience. No need to speak of cars and
trams and horses, smoke and grime. No need in fact, for words. Just let
the recorded sound be heard and they are there. Transported.
Actor But the scene is to be in an office, is it not? Why do we have
London's traffic flowing through an office?
Kipps Why indeed? Mr Bunce! (*He clicks his fingers again*)

*At once the traffic sound begins to fade and dissolves into the sonorous
ticking of a long-case clock*

Actor (*listening with a certain amount of awe*) Remarkable.

The clock fades out. The street sounds return

Kipps (*with a superior smile*) The miracle of science, the hands of Bunce.
He is particularly good at this sort of thing. And so to work. I am you,
you are your clerk. I enter briskly, you are already at work.
Actor (*preparing to perform*) You must forgive me, this is not ——
Kipps — your forte. Quite. And it won't become so unless you attempt
it. Begin. Just as we went through it all last night. (*Calling to the back
of the theatre*) I thank you!

The London street sound gives way to the sonorous clock

  Kipps exits

*The Actor, alias Tomes the clerk, stands working at a ledger. His desk
might be the stool, or a pile of boxes. Whatever, it suggests discomfort*

  Kipps enters briskly. He tosses his briefcase on to the desk and sits

*Kipps has learnt his part. The Actor struggles manfully, reading from the
manuscript. The conceit is that although the Actor is unaccomplished, his*

enthusiasm for the task will grow through the early part of the enactment, in spite of his protestations

A foul day, Tomes.

Tomes Yes, Mr Kipps. (*He sniffs*)

Kipps November. The drearest month of the year. Lowering to the spirits.

Tomes Yes, Mr Kipps. (*He sniffs*) This fog don't help.

Kipps (*looking up from his desk to address the audience*) The thickest of London pea-soupers. A yellow fog. A filthy, evil-smelling fog, a fog that choked and blinded, smeared and stained. I worked at some dull details of the conveyancing of property leases, forgetful for the moment of it pressing against the window like a furred beast at my back.

Tomes leaves his ledger, moves to Kipps's desk and knocks on it. Kipps looks up

Tomes Mr Bentley wishes to see you, sir.

Kipps Straight away?

Tomes Straight away, sir, if you would. (*He sniffs*)

Kipps (*addressing the audience*) That sniff, incidentally, occurred every twenty seconds, for which reason Tomes was confined, in general, to a cubbyhole in an outer lobby.

Kipps stands

Actor What now?

Kipps Now you become Bentley.

Actor Oh yes, of course. (*A beat*) Do I do all right? Will it pass?

Kipps Excellent. We'll make an Irving of ——

Actor (*angrily*) Will you be quiet about Irving!

Kipps Apologies. Carry on.

The Actor sits the other side of the desk from Kipps, becoming Mr Bentley as he does so. He polishes his glasses

Bentley Sit ye down, Arthur, sit ye down.

Kipps sits. Bentley spreads himself in a relaxed way, taking his time before he speaks

I don't think I ever told you about the extraordinary Mrs Drablow?

Kipps shakes his head

Mrs Drablow. (*He takes out her will and waves it at Kipps*) Mrs Alice Drablow of Eel Marsh House. Dead, don't you know.

Kipps Ah.

Bentley Yes. I inherited Mrs Drablow from my father. The family has had their business with this firm for ... oh ... (*He waves his hand, signifying ages*)

Kipps Oh yes?

Bentley A good age. Eighty-seven.

Kipps And it's her will you have there, I take it?

Bentley Mrs Drablow was, as they say, a rum 'un. Have you ever heard of the Nine Lives Causeway?

Kipps No, never.

Bentley Nor ever of Eel Marsh in ——shire?

That the written convention of "——shire" might be vocalized, I suggest that the actor mumbles and coughs through the "——"

Kipps No, sir.

Bentley Nor, I suppose, ever visited that county at all?

Kipps I'm afraid not.

Bentley Living there, anyone might become rum.

Kipps I've only a hazy idea of where it is.

Bentley Then, my boy, go home and pack your bags, and take the afternoon train from King's Cross, changing at Crewe and again at Homerby. From Homerby you take the branch line to the little market town of Crythin Gifford. After that, it's a wait for the tide!

Kipps The tide!

Bentley You can only cross the causeway at low tide. That takes you on to Eel Marsh and the house.

Kipps Mrs Drablow's?

Bentley When the tide comes in you're cut off until it's low again. Remarkable place. (*He stands to look out of the window*) Years since I went there, of course. My father took me. She didn't greatly care for visitors.

Kipps Was she a widow?

Bentley Since quite early in her marriage.

Kipps Children?

Bentley Children. (*He rubs at the window panes as a church bell tolls in the distance. He turns*) According to everything we've been told about Mrs Drablow, no, there were no children.

Kipps Did she have a great deal of money or land?

Bentley She owned her house, of course, and a few properties in Crythin Gifford — shops with tenants, that sort of thing; there's a poor sort of farm, half under water. And there are the usual small trusts and investments.

Kipps Then it all sounds pretty straightforward.

Bentley It does, does it not?

Kipps May I ask why I'm to go there?

Bentley To represent this firm at our client's funeral.

Kipps Oh yes, of course. I'll be very glad to go up to Mrs Drablow's funeral, naturally.

Bentley There's a bit more to it than that.

Kipps The will?

Bentley I'll let you have the details to read on your journey. But, principally, you're to go through Mrs Drablow's documents — her private papers ... whatever they may be. Wherever they may be ... and to bring them to this office.

Kipps I see.

Bentley Mrs Drablow was — somewhat ... disorganized, shall I say? It may take you a while.

Kipps A day or two?

Bentley At least a day or two, Arthur.

Kipps Will there be anyone there to help me?

Bentley I've made arrangements. There's a local man dealing with it all — he'll be in touch with you.

Kipps But presumably she had friends ... or even neighbours?

Bentley Eel Marsh House is far from any neighbour.

Kipps And being a rum 'un she never made friends, I suppose?

Bentley (*chuckling*) Come, Arthur, look on the bright side. Treat the whole thing as a jaunt.

Kipps stands

(*Waving his hand towards the window*) At least it'll take you out of all this for a day or two. You'll reach Crythin Gifford by late this evening, and there's a small hotel you can put up at for tonight. The funeral is tomorrow morning at eleven.

Bentley stands up and moves away from the desk

Kipps (*clearing the desk*) I had to inform my landlady that I would be away a couple of nights, and to scribble a note to my fiancée Stella, to whom I hoped to be married the following year. After that I was to catch the afternoon train to a remote corner of England of which, until a few moments ago, I had barely heard.

The Actor, now as Tomes, approaches Kipps with a thick brown envelope marked "Drablow"

Tomes The Drablow papers, sir.

Kipps Thank you. (*He takes them*) I must say, Tomes, for all it's a strange part of the world I'm going to, that it's a relief to be leaving this appalling fog and unhealthy atmosphere.

Tomes sniffs and goes. Pause. Kipps looks across at the Actor

(*Calling*) And you still feel unsure whether to go through with this?

Actor Oh, certainly.

Kipps In spite of having just performed as you have done?

Actor There are so many things we cannot represent. How do we represent the dog, the sea, the causeway? How the pony and trap?

Kipps With imagination, Mr Kipps. Our's, and our audience's.

Actor I would be obliged if you would inform me how imagination will create a pony and trap upon this stage.

Kipps, with alacrity, swings the skip into a position end on to the audience

Kipps Here, trap! (*Indicating the space in front of it*) Here, pony! What could be clearer?

A pause as the Actor surveys it dubiously

Actor It doesn't instantly say "trap" to me.

Kipps But you *ride* it, don't you? And with a whip! And with recorded sound of a pony's hooves, I promise, *nothing* in the *world* could say it clearer.

Actor Except a pony and trap.

Kipps Let us not be finicky, Mr Kipps.

Pause

Actor I have to own, the recorded sound is splendid. It was a great surprise to me.

Kipps And it does not stop now. There shall be more, much more. Tomorrow we are on the train. With more surprises. So now to work. (*He hands him some pages*) You will study these, I have divided up the lines again. And you will see I have cut much of the descriptive passages.

Actor But ——

Kipps Recorded sound, Mr Kipps. Recorded sound!

The Lights fade to Black-out. When they come up again, Kipps has a travelling bag, and from the sounds of steam trains and general bustle we are aware he is in King's Cross Station. The Actor reads from his manuscript now with more confidence

Actor Nothing could raise his spirits more than the sight of this great cavern of a railway station, glowing like the interior of a blacksmith's forge.

Kipps arranges his compartment and sits. He reads a newspaper

Beyond the windows it is quickly dark, and when the carriage blinds are down all is as cosy and enclosed as some lamplit study.

There are sounds of a steam train heading north. Kipps, in great contentment, reads his newspaper, and looks out of the window. After a while, the train slows down and draws to a halt as we hear "This is Crewe! Crewe Station! Passengers for Homerby please change here!" During the next speech, the Actor puts on a great-coat and hat

At Crewe he changes with ease,

Kipps swaps his seat

and continues on his way, noting that the track begins to veer towards
the east as well as heading north. It is only when he comes to change
again,

Kipps swaps his seat again

on to the branch line at the small station of Homerby, that he begins to
be less comfortable, for here the air is a great deal colder and blowing
in gusts from the east with an unpleasant rain upon its breath, and the
train in which he is to travel the last hour of his journey is ancient and
comfortless.

*Kipps turns up his collar and rubs his hands against the cold. The Actor
walks along the platform, sees Kipps, and climbs in by him as the guard's
whistle blows*

Kipps (*nodding*) It's a poor night.

*Samuel Daily nods agreement. The Actor is still reading at this stage,
though becoming freer in performance*

It seems I have exchanged one kind of poor weather for another. I left
London in the grip of an appalling fog, and up here it seems to be cold
enough for snow.

Sam Daily It's not snow. The wind'll blow itself out and take the rain off
with it by morning.

Kipps I'm very glad to hear it.

Sam Daily But if you think you've escaped the fogs by coming up here
you're mistaken. We get bad frets in this part of the world.

Kipps Frets?

Sam Daily Ay, frets. Sea-frets, sea-mists. They roll up in a minute from
the sea to land across the marshes. One minute it's as clear as a June day,
the next ... (*His gesture indicates the suddenness of the frets*) Terrible.
But if you're staying in Crythin you won't see the worst of it.

Kipps I stay there tonight, at the *Gifford Arms*. I expect to go out to see
something of the marshes later. (*He picks up his newspaper, nods at
Samuel Daily, and begins to read*)

The train puffs on a while

Sam Daily Mrs Drablow.

Kipps looks up at him

Drablow. (*He points at the envelope*)

Kipps nods

You don't tell me you're a relative.
Kipps I am her solicitor.
Sam Daily Ah! Bound for the funeral?
Kipps I am.
Sam Daily You'll be about the only one that is.
Kipps I gather she was something of a recluse? Well, that is sometimes
the way with old ladies. They turn inwards — grow eccentric. I suppose
it comes from living alone.
Sam Daily I daresay that it does, Mr ——?
Kipps Kipps. Arthur Kipps.
Sam Daily Samuel Daily.

They nod

And when you live alone in such a place as that it comes a good deal
easier.
Kipps (*smiling rather smugly*) Come, you're not going to start telling me
strange tales of lonely houses?

Pause

Sam Daily (*levelly*) No. I am not.

Pause. Kipps shudders

Kipps Well, all I can say is that it's a sad thing when someone lives for
eighty-seven years and can't count upon a few friendly faces to gather
together at their funeral. (*He rubs his hand on the window and peers out*)
How far have we to go?
Sam Daily (*looking through the window*) Twelve miles. It's a far flung
part of the world. We don't get many visitors.

Kipps I suppose because there is nothing much to see.

Sam Daily It all depends what you mean by "nothing". (*Pause*) But you'll find everything hospitable enough at Crythin, for all it's a plain little place. We tuck ourselves in with our backs to the wind, and carry on with our business. (*He takes a card from his wallet and hands it to Kipps*) Should you need anyone ...

Kipps Thank you. I doubt I shall. Whatever practical help I need I'm sure the local agent will provide — and I don't intend to be here more than a day or two.

Daily looks at him in silence

But thanks all the same. (*He puts the card into his waistcoat pocket*)

The train swells to a crescendo as the Lights fade to a Black-out, then, as it whistles, snaps off. When the Lights come up again, Kipps is arranging the furniture: making a hotel lounge. The Actor has moved to the side of the stage and is donning an apron

The *Gifford Arms* was as comfortable a hotel as I could have wished to find.

Kipps looks around him approvingly, settles in an armchair and holds his hands to the fire. There is a murmur of voices from the public bar

My spirits rose and I began to feel more like a man on holiday than one come to attend a funeral. (*He takes out notepaper and pen and begins to write*) My Dearest Stella ——

But at this the Landlord enters to interrupt him

Landlord Are you a friend of Mr Daily's, then, sir?

Kipps No, no.

Landlord Ah. Not meaning to pry, only I saw you arrive in his car.

Kipps I met him on the train. He was kind enough to bring me from the station.

Landlord I see. He's a large landowner is Mr Daily. Buying up half the county.

Kipps In that case I may be doing business with him myself before the year is out. I am a solicitor looking after the affairs of Mrs Alice Drablow of Eel Marsh House. Perhaps you knew of her?

Landlord (*a momentary reaction which he quickly controls*) I knew of her.

Kipps It's quite possible that her estate will come up for sale in due course.

Landlord I doubt whether even Samuel Daily would go so far.

Kipps I don't think I fully understand you. I gather there is a farm a few miles out of the town.

Landlord (*dismissively*) Hoggetts! Fifty acres and half of it under flood for the best part of the year. Hoggetts is nothing.

Kipps There's also Eel Marsh House and all the land surrounding it — would that be practicable for farming?

Landlord No, sir.

Kipps Well, might not Mr Daily simply want to add a little more to his empire? You imply he is that kind of man.

Landlord Maybe he is. But let me tell you that you won't find anybody, not even Mr Sam Daily having to do with any of it. I'll wish you good-night, sir. We can serve breakfast at any time in the morning, to your convenience.

The Landlord abruptly leaves Kipps. A moment, then Kipps resumes his letter. We hear his words as a voice-over — his tone is slightly tetchy

Kipps's voice There seems to be a propensity for leaving conversations to hang in the air whenever Mrs Drablow's name is mentioned. People close up, change the subject or leave the room. I suppose it's inevitable: these small, out of the way communities have only themselves to look to for whatever drama and mystery they can extract out of life. And I would think it not unfair to say that country people, particularly those who inhabit the remoter corners of our island, are rather more supersti-tious, more gullible, more slow-witted perhaps — certainly more unsophisticated — than those of us who encounter the "metropolitan experience" every day. Doubtless in such a place as this, with its eerie marshes, sudden fogs, moaning winds and lonely houses, any poor old woman might be looked at askance; once upon a time, after all, she would have been branded as a witch ...

The Lights cross-fade to the worker state. Kipps, no longer acting, sits in a chair, and talks across to the Actor

Kipps Admit it, Mr Kipps, secretly you are enjoying this.

Actor I am very grateful to you for your assistance. I cannot say I am enjoying it.

Kipps Mr Kipps, every day you have come here you have grown in stature and confidence.

Actor But this is merely practice. What you call rehearsal. I fear it will be different altogether before an audience.

Kipps Mr Kipps, sir!

Actor Yes?

Kipps For all you deny it, you damn well *will* be an Irving! Now then, tomorrow I should like to work right through to the end.

Actor In one?

Kipps If we are able. How does that seem?

Actor I have a horror of it. Watching you, it is as if I relive it all, moment by moment ... though you, of course, will never suffer as I did — I must always tell myself that.

Kipps moves to him and gently takes his hand

Kipps But never think I don't feel for you. I have a child myself.

Actor You have?

Kipps A daughter. She is four.

Actor And well? And happy?

Kipps I thank Providence.

Actor (*earnestly gripping Kipps's hand*) Love her. Take care of her. (*A pause as he looks into Kipps's eyes*) Well — tomorrow. Yes. Let us work to the end. And, all being well, tomorrow *I* shall have a surprise for *you*.

Kipps Excellent! You have a theatrical's instincts, Mr Kipps, if not his enthusiasm. Till tomorrow then!

Kipps moves to go as the Lights fade to Black-out

The Lights come up to suggest the dawning of a crisp, clear day, and we hear the hubbub of the market place as Kipps attaches a black armband to his sleeve. The Actor, as Mr Jerome, comes up to Kipps. Like Kipps, he wears a black tie and armband. The Actor has learnt his words and is no longer reading

Jerome Mr Kipps?

Kipps Yes indeed.

Jerome (*offering his hand*) Mr Jerome. Your agent here.

Kipps Of course. How d'you do.

Jerome I trust you spent a comfortable night?

Kipps I can't remember when I've slept so well.

Jerome Good, good. It's a sad business, that brings you here.

Kipps Yes. Of course, I never met Mrs Drablow ——

Jerome No. Of course. I don't wish to hurry you, Mr Kipps, but if we were to step out now we'd be about right for time.

Kipps Ah yes, of course.

They step into the sunshine. Now the market noises intensify. Kipps looks about him

I must say, my first impressions of your little town are entirely favourable, Mr Jerome.

Jerome It's a busy day for us, market day. They come from all over.

Kipps Though I'd like to experience it in happier circumstances. Our funeral garb seems at odds with the prevailing mood of the place.

The market noises lull

(*looking about him*) Is it my imagination, or are we the subject of scrutiny, Mr Jerome?

Jerome doesn't reply

There! Those men — did you see? They turned away then they caught my eye ... and there!

Jerome (*walking away*) It's only a short walk to the graveyard, Mr Kipps.

Kipps (*following and looking back over his shoulder*) I feel like some pariah.

Jerome doesn't speak

Oh well. (*He smiles*) I suppose we must look like a pair of gloomy ravens amongst all this, mustn't we? You and I, Mr Jerome, are the spectres at the feast.

He smiles across at Jerome who doesn't acknowledge him. The market

*hubbub fades, and now their footsteps echo as they walk. The Lights dim
slightly, as if filtered through spreading trees. They walk on*

I take it she is to be buried in the churchyard?
Jerome That is so, yes.
Kipps Is there a family grave?

Jerome glances as Kipps closely

Jerome *(after a pause)* No. At least not here, not in this churchyard.
Kipps Somewhere else?
Jerome It is ... no longer in use. The area is unsuitable.
Kipps *(stopping walking; turning to Jerome)* I'm afraid I don't quite
    understand ——

*But Jerome carries on walking. The Lights suggest the interior of the
church as we hear the following voice-over*

Priest's voice I know that my Redeemer liveth, and that he shall stand at
    the latter day upon the earth. And though after my skin worms destroy
    this body, yet in my flesh shall I see God: whom I shall see for myself,
    and mine eyes shall behold, and not another.

*This is followed by the echoing tread of the undertaker's men bearing the
coffin down the aisle. Both Kipps and Jerome turn upstage. The voice-over
fades in again with the Priest's voice*

Behold, I show you a mystery. We shall not all sleep, but we shall all be
changed, in a moment, in the twinkling of an eye, at the last trump, (for
the trumpet shall sound) and the dead shall be raised incorruptible, and
we shall be changed.

As the voice-over continues, Kipps looks back into the audience

*In the centre aisle stands the Woman in Black. Her clothes are black,
old-fashioned. She wears a black bonnet that partly obscures her face,
though, from what remains of it to be seen, it appears she suffers from
some terrible wasting disease. She is extremely pale, the thinnest layer
of flesh is tautly stretched across her bones, and her eyes seem sunken
back into her head*

*Kipps is clearly momentarily shocked to see her, then steadies himself.
The Actor does not look back at her, and we can believe he does not see
her, nor know she's there*

For this corruptible must put on incorruption, and this mortal shall have
put on immortality. So when this corruptible shall have put on
incorruption, and this mortal shall have put on immortality, then shall
be brought to pass the saying that is written, Death is swallowed up in
victory. O death, where is there thy sting? O grave, where is thy victory?

Kipps pulls his eyes away from her

As he turns away, so she moves back down the aisle

But thanks be to God, which giveth us the victory through our Lord Jesus
Christ. Therefore, my beloved brethren, be ye steadfast, unmoveable,
always abounding in the work of the Lord, for as much as ye know that
your labour is not in vain in the Lord.

*The church gives way to the graveyard. Jerome and Kipps stand as if
looking into the grave, over the edge of the stage. Birdsong is heard,
dissolving once again into the Priest's voice*

Man that is born of woman hath but a short time to live, and is full of
misery. He cometh up, and is cut down, like a flower; he fleeth as it were
a shadow, and never continueth in one stay.

The Woman in Black enters behind the two of them, upstage

In the midst of life we are in death: of whom may we seek for succour,
but of thee, O Lord, who for our sins art justly displeased.

*Kipps, sensing her presence, looks around. Again the Actor does not see
her*

For as much as it hath pleased Almighty God of his great mercy to take
unto himself the soul of our dear sister here departed, we therefore
commit her body to the ground; earth to earth, ashes to ashes, dust to
dust.

*The voice-over fades down. Kipps turns away from the Woman in Black
and kneels to pray fervently at the graveside*

　The Woman in Black moves away

*The voice-over dissolves into birdsong. At length, Kipps crosses himself
and steps back from the grave*

Kipps A very poignant ceremony.

Jerome is silent

　Tell me, that woman ... I hope she can find her own way home ... she
　looked so dreadfully unwell. Who was she?

Jerome looks at him

　The young woman with the wasted face, behind you in the church and
　then in the graveyard here, a few yards from us.
Jerome A *young* woman?
Kipps Yes, yes, with the skin stretched over her bones, I could scarcely
　bear to look at her ... she was tall, she wore a bonnet type of hat ... I
　suppose to try and conceal as much as she could of her face, poor thing.

Jerome looks frozen, pale, his throat moving as if he were unable to utter

　Is there anything the matter? You look unwell.
Jerome (*at length; in a low voice*) I did not see a young woman.
Kipps But surely ... (*He turns*)

　The Woman in Black appears again

　(*Pointing*) Look, there she is again ... ought we not to ——

*Jerome grabs his wrist, evidently in an extreme of terror. He avoids
looking where Kipps is pointing. Kipps looks at him in astonishment*

　The Woman in Black goes

(*At length*) Mr Jerome, can you take my arm ... I would be obliged if you
would loosen your grip a little ... if you can just walk a few steps, back
to the church ... path ... I saw a bench there, a little way inside the gate,
you can rest and recover while I go for help ... a car ...

Jerome (*almost shrieking*) No!

Kipps But my dear man!

Jerome No. I apologize ... (*He takes deep breaths*) I am so sorry. It was
nothing ... a passing faintness ... it will be best if you would just walk
back with me towards my offices in Penn Street, off the square.

Kipps If you are sure ——

Jerome Quite sure. Come ...

Kipps You quite worried me just now, I ——

Jerome Please, I apologize. It was nothing. Nothing at all.

Kipps (*after a pause*) Very well. (*Pause*) I gather you are to take me over
to Eel Marsh House later?

Jerome (*stiffly*) No. I shall not go there. You can cross any time after one
o'clock. Keckwick will come for you. He has always been the go-
between to that place. I take it you have a key?

Kipps nods

You will find Mr Keckwick perfectly obliging.

Kipps Good.

Jerome Though not very communicative.

Kipps (*smiling*) Oh, I'm getting very used to that.

*Kipps clicks his fingers towards the back of the theatre. The Lights change
to the worker state again*

I'm sorry, Mr Kipps, I have to stop. (*He shakes the Actor's hand, looking
fervently into his eyes*) You said you had a surprise for me — I had no
idea, *no idea*, it would be that.

Actor No?

Kipps That was the most — remarkable — *coup de théâtre* I have ever
experienced.

The Actor is changing into a greatcoat, cap and high riding boots

Actor No, really?

Kipps I am devastated. Devastated. How did you manage it?

Actor Well, I worked hard, I suppose. As you said: time and tears. (*He smiles*)

Kipps But — from *nowhere*, Mr Kipps — it was miraculous! How on earth did you set about it?

Actor Oh ——

Kipps No. Very well. I understand. One must appreciate the magic, one must not ask how the magic works. But I do appreciate it. (*He pumps the Actor's hand*) I assure you, sir, *I do*! Quite, quite remarkable — and terrifying!

Actor (*a little puzzled*) Well, you're very kind, sir.

Kipps And you, sir, are a true theatrical.

The Actor modestly reacts. A pause

Do we proceed?

Actor If you wish.

Kipps And will there be more — surprises?

Actor I will do my very best, though I cannot be altogether confident.

Kipps gives the Actor's hand a final fervent shake then signals to the back of the theatre. The Lights revert to a performance state. There is the sound effect of a pony and trap as Kipps puts on more relaxed clothes. When dressed, the Actor picks up a riding whip, places the skip end on to the audience, and sits facing out front. Kipps looks at him as we hear the pony draw to a halt and the Actor, as Keckwick, reins in. Kipps, after digesting the sight a moment, turns away as if looking for a car

Keckwick (*at length*) Mr Kipps?

Kipps (*turning to him*) Yes?

Keckwick says nothing, looks ahead

You aren't — you're not Mr Keckwick by any chance?

Keckwick nods

Oh, that's delightful — I was expecting a car!

Kipps climbs up behind Keckwick who clucks at the pony, which then sets off

(*As the trap is under way*) This is a remarkable corner of the world, Mr Keckwick. (*He looks about him with evident pleasure*) Sky, sky, and only a strip of land. This must be how those great landscape painters saw Holland, or the area around Norwich, don't you think?

Keckwick does not respond

No clouds at all today, though I can imagine how magnificently that huge brooding area of sky would look with grey, scudding rain and storm clouds lowering over the estuary.

They drive on a while in silence, Kipps continuing to gaze about him

It is quite startlingly beautiful, the wide, bare openness of it. This sense of space, the vastness of the sky — I would have travelled a thousand miles to see this. I have never imagined such a place!

They trot on, the silence broken by nothing but the sound of the pony, and occasional, harsh, weird cries from birds. Kipps kneels up on the skip, alert, looking ahead

And that, I take it, is the Nine Lives Causeway!

The Lights isolate Kipps and we hear the pony and trap as it rolls across

Ahead, the water gleamed like metal, lying only shallowly over the sand. A narrow track led directly forwards, and I saw how, when the tide came in, it would quickly be submerged and untraceable. Then I looked up ahead, and saw as if rising out of the water itself, a tall, gaunt house of grey stone with a slate roof.

The Lights come up on stage. Keckwick reins in the pony and dismounts

It stood like some lighthouse or beacon or Martello tower, the most astonishingly situated house I had ever seen or could ever conceivably have imagined — isolated, uncompromising, but also, I

thought, handsome. For a moment or two, I simply sat looking about me
in amazement. I felt a strange sensation, an excitement mingled with
alarm ... But I was not afraid — of what could I be afraid in this rare and
beautiful spot? The wind? The marsh birds crying? Reeds and still
water? (*Suddenly he moves to Keckwick*) How long will the causeway
remain passable?

Keckwick Till five.

Kipps Listen. It will be quite ridiculous for you to be driving to and fro
twice a day. The best thing will be for me to bring my bags and some
food and drink and stay a couple of nights here. That way I shall finish
the business a good deal more efficiently and you will not be troubled.
I'll return with you later this afternoon and then, tomorrow, perhaps you
could bring me back as early as possible, according to the tides.

A considerable pause until Keckwick nods his agreement

Or perhaps you would prefer to wait here for me now, though I shall be
a couple of hours. You know what suits you best.

*For reply, Keckwick climbs on to the skip and flicks his whip. We hear the
pony's hooves across the gravel, fading into the distance. The Lights
isolate Keckwick, and gradually fade, along with the pony's hooves. The
Actor climbs off the skip as the Lights bounce back. He takes off his cap
and undoes his coat as he speaks*

Actor And so, imagine if you would, this stage an island, this aisle a
causeway, running like a ribbon from the salt marsh through the sea, the
only link between the gaunt, grey house and land. Imagine Arthur Kipps
alone there now, a tiny figure, lost in the immensity and wideness of
marsh and sky, dwarfed by the house, alone amid the mysterious
shimmering beauty. He feels the key in his pocket, but does not go
inside. Instead, he walks away from the house towards the fragmentary
ruins of some old church or chapel. To the west, on his right hand, the
sun is already beginning to slip down in a great, wintry, golden-red ball;
to the east, sea and sky have darkened slightly to a uniform, leaden grey.

*Kipps scrambles across the skip and through the gauze. The Lights reveal
the shrouded furniture. A sudden, harsh cry from a bird startles him. We
hear its loudly beating wings and the echo of its cry among the ruins. Kipps
watches it fly away*

Imagine now, a burial ground. Imagine fifty gravestones, most of them leaning or completely fallen, covered in lichens, mosses, scoured pale by the salt wind, stained by years of driving rain. Names and dates are now barely decipherable. Imagine him grown conscious of the cold, the bleakness and eeriness of the spot, decide to leave, to go back to the house, to switch on a good many lights, to light a fire. Now see him turn ...

Kipps turns

The Woman in Black appears ahead of him

Involuntarily, Kipps steps back a pace or two, then stands as if frozen. The Woman in Black is amongst what we think of as the gravestones. It is not clear that she stares at Kipps, nor that she doesn't

The moment is held in silence, then the Woman slips away and out of sight

As soon as she does, Kipps rushes after her to look the way she's gone. He stands at the exit, searching with his eyes, then at length moves back through the gauze. The Actor, meanwhile, has not looked upstage

Kipps Beyond the wall the grass gave way within a yard or two to sand and shallow water. The marshes and the salt flats stretched away until they merged with the rising tide. I could see for *miles*. There was no sign *at all* of the woman in black, nor *any* place in which she could have concealed herself.

Silence

I did not believe in ghosts.

There is the sound effect of Kipps running, the thud of his footsteps, the panting of his breath

Actor By the time he reaches the house he is in a lather of sweat from his exertions and the extremes of his emotions.

We hear the door of the house slam shut

For a long time he does not move from the dark, wood-panelled hall. He wants company, and he has none. He wants lights. He needs reassurance. But more than anything else, he needs an *explanation*. (*Pause*) For he does not believe in ghosts.

Kipps But out on the marshes just now, I saw a woman who — whose form was quite substantial, yet — Oh God — I cannot describe it — I ... (*He moves to sit. He takes a moment to compose himself*) The expression on her face ... desperate, yearning malevolence ... filled me with indescribable loathing and fear. And she vanished in a way that no living human being could possibly manage to do. (*Pause*) I did not believe in ghosts.

A clock begins to strike, deep in the house

Actor What other explanation is there?

Pause

Kipps (*moving about the stage, visibly putting the experience behind him*) Hall, staircase, kitchen, scullery. (*He switches on a light. The bulb is weak*) Drawing-room, sitting-room, dining-room, study.

Actor Nothing unpleasant, no shades of Miss Havisham, no rubbish piled in corners, no half-starved dogs or cats. A damp, musty, sweet-sour smell there is — but is that remarkable in a house situated as is this one? Furniture — good, solid, dark, old-fashioned. Books, pictures, bureaux.

Kipps opens the skip and takes out bundles of documents, scattering them about him as the Actor speaks

Bureaux. Desks, writing-tables, bureaux. Papers, papers, in bundles, in boxes, letters, receipts, legal documents, notebooks, papers. All of which he must examine. A huge task, and one which there is little point in starting now, it is too late and he is too unnerved.

We see Kipps find a bottle of brandy, which he considers opening, then replaces

Kipps (*looking up from the skip*) How one old woman had endured day after day, night after night in this house I could not conceive. I should have gone mad.

Actor He decides to leave the place till the following morning. It will be an hour before Keckwick returns, and if he steps out well he will be back in Crythin Gifford in time to save him from turning out. The causeway is still visible, the roads back are straight and he cannot possibly lose himself.

Kipps switches off the Lights and locks up. Again the sound of the door slamming shut

Imagine him now, striding ahead, small and insignificant in that vast landscape. As he walks he summons up the image of the black-robed figure ——

Kipps looks back over his shoulder

—persuades himself she had not vanished as he'd thought, but that there must have been some slope or dip into which she had concealed herself. For he does not believe in ghosts. He puts her from his mind, walks on, struck by the absolute indifference of sky and water to his presence. Then, from this reverie, he becomes aware he cannot see for more than a few yards ahead,

Kipps registers this in the dimming light. He turns

and that behind him Eel Marsh House is quite invisible.

Kipps A thick, damp, sea-mist. Damp, clinging, cobwebby, fine and impenetrable. The sea-fret Mr Daily talked of.

Actor He must turn, retrace his steps to the house, and wait till Keckwick comes for him.

The Lights have dimmed to virtual darkness

Kipps The mist was salty, light and pale and moving in front of my eyes all the time. I felt confused, teased by it, as though it were made up of millions of live fingers that crept over me, hung on to me and then shifted away again.

Actor Step by slow step he goes, baffled by the moving, shifting mist, praying to reach the house. A nightmare walk, until ...

Fade up sound of a pony and trap. Kipps turns in evident relief, as the sound fades down, changes its apparent direction, swirls and fades as if carried on the mist

Kipps Keckwick!

The sound grows near, then recedes. Kipps is baffled by it, at one moment seems to locate it in the fog, at the next is utterly disorientated. At length, the noise of the pony and trap fades altogether, and away on the marsh is a draining, sucking, churning sound, which goes on, together with the shrill neighing and whinnying of a horse in panic. And then another cry: a shout, a terrified sobbing — it is hard to decipher, though it is clear it comes from a young child. Kipps struggles blindly forward a few steps

Oh no — oh no ... (*Screaming out*) No! No! No! *Keckwick!*

Black-out. In the darkness, we hear the front door slam. When the Lights return, Kipps is on stage in the house, clearly in shock. From the skip he takes out the bottle of brandy and a glass and pours himself a largish measure. He sits for a moment. He jumps up and feverishly starts to walk about the house again, rummaging through rooms and furniture

Actor In despair and fearfulness he goes about the house, switching on every light he can make work — in the vain hope that their glow might be seen across the misty wasteland.
Kipps (*pacing restlessly*) Every door was open, every room orderly, dusty, bitterly cold and damp and yet also somehow stifling.

Kipps arrives at the closed door. He stops

Actor One door is locked.
Kipps At the far end of a passage that led away from three bedrooms on the second floor. There was no keyhole, no bolt on the outside. (*He rattles it and kicks at it angrily, beating it with his fists. Then, as his anger subsides, he slides, sobbing, to the floor*)

The Actor is now dressed as Keckwick. He stands at the foot of the steps, as the doorbell rings. Kipps slowly comes out of his sleep, evidently unrefreshed, stiff in his limbs, staggering to answer the bell. The light

outside is now full moonlight which shines on to the causeway and the
actors. Kipps, on seeing Keckwick, seems bewildered

Keckwick You have to wait for a fret like that to clear itself. There's no
crossing over while a fret's up. Unlucky for you that was. And after that
there's the wait for the tide. Awkward place. You'll be finding that out
fast enough.

Kipps What time is it?

Keckwick Nigh on two.

Kipps I wouldn't have expected you to come back at this hour. It's very
good of you.

Keckwick I wouldn't have left you over the night. Wouldn't have done
that to you.

Kipps (*suddenly*) But what happened to you, how do you manage to be
here — *how did you get out?*

Keckwick looks a long moment into Kipps's face. Then he climbs on the
trap once more. Kipps climbs up. We hear the pony and trap set off

(*As he is carried on the trap*) I fell into a sort of trance, half sleeping, half
waking, rocked by the motion of the cart. I knew I had entered some
hitherto unimagined realm of consciousness and there was no going
back. That the woman by the graves had been ghostly I now — not
believed, no *knew*, for certainty lay deep within me. And I began to
suspect that the pony and trap, the pony and trap with the child who had
cried out so terribly and which had been sucked into the quicksands,
they too had not been real, not there, present, not substantial, but ghostly
also. What I had heard, I had heard as clearly as I now heard the roll of
the cart and the drumming of the pony's hooves, and what I had seen —
the woman with the pale, wasted face, by the grave of Mrs Drablow and
again in the old burial ground — I had seen. I would have sworn that on
oath. Yet they had been, in some sense I did not understand, unreal,
ghostly; things that were dead.

CURTAIN

ACT II

There is the sound of the busy market town

The Actor, as Jerome, sits working at his desk

Kipps enters and knocks on his door

Jerome answers, evidently with reluctance

Kipps Mr Jerome.
Jerome Ah. Yes. (*At length*) Won't you, er — won't you come in?
Kipps (*stepping in*) I trust you are fully recovered — after your experience at Mrs Drablow's funeral?
Jerome Thank you, yes. Thank you.

Silence

Kipps No doubt you're wondering why I'm here.

Jerome doesn't respond

You see, I had no idea — I don't know whether you had — of the volume of papers belonging to Mrs Drablow. Tons of the stuff and most of it, I've no doubt, so much waste, but it will have to be gone through item by item, nevertheless. It seems that, unless I am able to take up residence in Crythin Gifford for the foreseeable future, I shall have to have some help.

Jerome's expression is one of panic. He shifts his chair back, away from Kipps

Jerome I'm afraid I can't offer you help, Mr Kipps. Oh no.
Kipps I wasn't thinking that you would do anything personally, but perhaps you have a young assistant.

Jerome There is no-one. I am quite on my own. I cannot give any help at all.

Kipps Well then, help me to find someone. Surely the town will yield me a young man with a modicum of intelligence, and keen to earn a few pounds, whom I may take on for the job?

Jerome (*in great agitation*) I'm sorry — this is a small place — young people leave — there are no openings.

Kipps But I am offering an opening — albeit temporary.

Jerome (*almost shouting*) You will find no-one suitable!

Pause

Kipps (*very calmly and quietly*) Mr Jerome, what you mean is not that there is no-one available, that no young person — or older person for that matter — could be found. You are backing away from speaking the truth of the matter, which is that I should not find a soul willing to spend any time out at Eel Marsh House, for fear of the stories about that place proving true — for fear of encountering what I have already encountered.

Silence. At length, Jerome, in great agitation, moves to look out of the window, his back to Kipps

Jerome Keckwick came back for you.

Kipps Yes. I was more grateful than I can say.

Jerome There's nothing Keckwick doesn't know about Eel Marsh House.

Kipps Do I take it he fetched and carried sometimes for Mrs Drablow?

Jerome (*nodding*) She saw no-one else. Not ... (*he stops*)

Kipps (*evenly*) Not another living soul.

Pause

Jerome There are stories. Tales. There's all that nonsense. You can discount most of it.

Kipps Of course. But not all.

Jerome You saw that woman in the churchyard.

Kipps I saw her again. In that old burial ground.

Jerome turns suddenly to face Kipps, clearly most distressed by the conversation. Kipps decides to spare his feelings

Well, I'm not going to be put out by a ghost or several ghosts, Mr Jerome. My work has to be done. And I doubt if the woman in black can have any animosity towards me. I wonder who she was? Is? (*He laughs unnaturally*) I hardly know how to refer to her!

Silence

I must face it out, Mr Jerome. Such things one must face.
Jerome So I said. So I said — once.

The Lights lose Jerome. Kipps looks with concern towards the Actor, who, in agitation, is dressing as Sam Daily once again. Kipps moves to him

Kipps Mr Kipps, are you all right?
Actor I — yes. Yes, I am. Jerome was terrified.
Kipps (*bringing him into the light*) But you, yourself — if would seem you are in a — a state of emotion ...
Actor (*a trace of panic in his voice*) I was. I was. My emotions had become so volatile and so extreme, that I was living in another dimension. My heart seemed to beat faster, my step to be quicker, everything I saw was brighter, its outlines more sharply, precisely defined, I ... (*he stops*)

Kipps looks at him, evidently anxious

Kipps Can you go on?
Actor Yes.
Kipps Can you go on until the end?
Actor Oh yes. Yes, I must. Let us go on. Let us have done with it for God's sake!

He takes a few deep breaths and composes himself. Kipps approaches him

Kipps Mr Daily!
Sam Daily Mr Kipps! How's things with you?
Kipps Very well, I thank you.
Sam Daily And your business?

Kipps Mrs Drablow's estate? Oh, I shall soon have all that in order. Though I confess there will be rather more to do than I had anticipated.

Sam Daily You have been out to the house?

Kipps Certainly.

Sam Daily Ah.

Pause

Kipps To tell the truth I'm enjoying myself. I am finding the whole thing rather a challenge.

A long pause as Daily regards Kipps. Kipps shifts uneasily and glances away

Sam Daily Mr Kipps, you are whistling in the dark. You're a fool if you go on with it.

Kipps If you mean you think I should give up the job I've been sent here to do and turn tail and run ——

Sam Daily Listen to me, Arthur. I'm not going to fill you up with a lot of women's tales ... you'd find those out fast enough if you ask about the place. Maybe you already have?

Kipps No. Only hints — and Mr Jerome turning a little pale.

Sam Daily But you went out there to the house.

Kipps I went there and I had an experience I shouldn't care to go through again, though I confess I can't explain it. It seems to me, Mr Daily, that I have seen whatever ghost haunts Eel Marsh. A woman in black with a wasted face. Because I have no doubt at all that she was what people call a ghost, that she was not a real, living, breathing, human being. Well, she did me no harm. She neither spoke nor came near me. I did not like her look and I like the — the power that seemed to emanate from her towards me even less, but I have convinced myself that it is a power that cannot do more than make me feel afraid. If I go there and see her again, I am prepared.

Sam Daily And the pony and trap?

Silence

Kipps So you know of that. (*At length*) I won't run away.

Sam Daily You shouldn't go there.

Kipps I'm afraid I'm going.

Sam Daily You shouldn't go there alone.

Kipps It seems I can find no-one to come with me.

Sam Daily No. And you will not.

Kipps Good God, man, Mrs Drablow lived alone there for — what was it? — sixty-odd years, to a ripe old age. She must have come to terms with all the ghosts about the place.

Sam Daily Ay. Maybe that's just what she did do. (*Pause*) But you're set on it?

Kipps I am.

Sam Daily Then take a dog.

Kipps (*laughing*) I haven't got a dog.

Sam Daily I have. (*He whistles, then bends and pats the "dog"*) Take her. Bring her back when you are done.

Kipps Will she come with me?

Sam Daily She'll do what I tell her.

Kipps pets her

Kipps What's her name?

Sam Daily Spider.

Kipps All right, I'll be glad of her company, I confess. Thank you. Come, girl! Spider!

Kipps and the "dog" move out of the light

Actor (*loosening his "Daily" clothes*) Next morning, he crosses to the house on a bicycle lent him by his landlord. The little dog Spider bounds behind. The sun is high, the very air seems purified and more exhilarating.

Kipps There they lay, those glittering, beckoning, silver marshes. I could hear the mysterious silence, and once again the haunting, strange beauty of it all aroused a response deep within me. I could not run away from that place. I had fallen under some sort of spell of the kind that certain places exude and it drew me, my imaginings, my longings, my curiosity, my whole spirit, towards itself.

The Lights suggest the house interior. The Actor moves to the side of the stage, to a position as physically removed from Kipps as possible — perhaps even to the body of the theatre

Actor He lights fires, airs sheets and blankets, opens windows, draws up
blinds, and sets himself to work in one of the bays of the morning-room.

*Kipps starts sorting the letters into piles — those to be dealt with, those to
discard*

Kipps Well, Spider, have you ever seen a more worthless collection of
papers? I do believe Mrs Drablow kept every bill, receipt and Christmas
card she ever had. (*He fondles Spider*) There's even shopping lists,
would you believe!
Actor It was pretty tedious going, but he persevered patiently enough,
untying and cursorily examining bundle after bundle of worthless old
papers before tossing them aside.

*Kipps works on a moment, then yawns and stretches. He stands, crosses
the stage and we hear the door slam. He whistles for the dog*

Kipps (*calling*) Spider! Spider — rabbits! (*He moves through the gauze
into the old graveyard*) Last time I was here, among these graves, I saw
a woman. (*He bends to the dog*) Where is she, Spider! Where is she, girl!
(*He pats the dog, then stoops to decipher an inscription*) In Loving
Memory ... Something net ... Humfrye ... nineteen o-something ... and
of her something ... something iel Drablow ... (*He contemplates the
stone a moment, then whistles the dog*) Spider!
Actor He returns to the house and to his task. Already the air is turning
colder, the sky losing its light.

We hear the door slam as Kipps returns to his papers

On into the evening he works. Spider is an excellent companion and he
is glad of her gentle breathing, her occasional scratching or clattering
about in that big empty house. But his main sensation is one of tedium
and a certain lethargy combined with a desire to finish the job and be
back in London with his dear Stella.

*Kipps sorts through the papers, discarding many, saving few, as the
Lights fade. When they return, he is in the process of clearing his work
for the night, putting things in piles on the floor*

Kipps Another day or two and we'll be done. It's time for bed. Come, Spider!

He moves by a circuitous route to his bed. He lies down, covering himself with a blanket he has found amongst the clutter. Before the Lights go down, he reaches down to fondle the dog

Would Mr Daily let me take you home with me to London? I wonder. You'd like Stella. I'm not sure you'd like London. Good-night now. Good-night.

And the Lights fade to a Black-out. Suddenly, they return, via a shaft of moonlight, and Kipps sits immediately upright. Silence

(*At length, whispering*) What is it, Spider? What is it?

Silence. Then, from the depths of the house, comes a sound like an intermittent bump or rumble. Kipps listens, frozen. At length, it stops. Slowly, he climbs out of bed

(*Whispering*) Good girl, good girl ... (*he moves away from his bed*)

The sound begins again. Kipps moves cautiously through the house. As he does, the moonlight appears and disappears through the many windows. Gradually, the sound gets louder as Kipps gets nearer, until, inevitably, he's drawn to the closed door. The sound is at its loudest now. Kipps has not the courage to try the door, though it's evident that the source of the sound is behind it. He stands as if paralysed outside. Then, from out on the marshes, comes the sound of a child's cry. Kipps swings around to listen

Actor He gropes his way back to his bedroom, and looks out. There lie the marshes, silver gray and empty, there is the water of the estuary, flat as a mirror with the full moon lying upturned upon it.
Kipps But nothing. No-one. The slightest of breezes, nothing more.

The distant rumble from the room has now ceased. In silence, Kipps moves back through the house, towards the room with the closed door. He reaches it, there is no sound now. He puts his hand on to the handle, hesitates, then turns it. It does not give. He pushes against it slightly with his shoulder. Nothing. Slowly, the dawn light filters up

Actor In the morning he awakes to a change in the weather. When he looks out he can hardly see the division between land and water, water and sky. All is a uniform grey, with low, thick cloud and a drizzle.

Kipps I cycled back to Crythin, Spider bounding behind me. There was a letter from Stella, full of exclamations of regret at my absence, and pride in my responsibility. I had the landlord's wife refill my hamper, purchased a good strong torch, and with the letter warming my inside pocket, cycled back, whistling as I went.

Actor He works through the day, clearing paper after paper, then, after supper, as a diversion, begins to read some letters he has found.

Kipps (*sitting with a slim packet of documents and letters*) They were dated between a February of about sixty years ago and the summer of the following year. They were sent first from the manor house of a village some twenty miles from here, and later from a lodge in Scotland. All were addressed to "My dear" or "Dearest Alice" and signed for the most part "J", but occasionally "Jennet". The writer, a young woman and apparently a relative of Mrs Drablow, was unmarried and with child. At first, she was still living at home with her parents; later, she was sent away.

Actor In Scotland, a son is born to her and she writes of him with a desperate clinging affection. Pressure is being put on her to give up the child for adoption; she refuses, saying over and over again that they will never be parted.

As Kipps speaks the following, he is joined by the voice-over of a young woman speaking the same words. They speak the first sentences in unison, then Kipps leaves it to the voice-over

Kipps		"He is mine. Why should I not have
Young Woman's	(*together*)	what is mine? He shall not go to stran-
voice		gers. I shall kill us both before I let him go."

Actor And then the tone changes.

Young Woman's voice "What else can I do? I am quite helpless. If you and Morgan are to have him I shall mind it less. I suppose it must be."

Actor But the last letter of all is written in a very small, cramped hand.

Young Woman's voice "Love him, take care of him as your own. But he is mine, mine, he can never be yours. Oh, forgive me. I think my heart will break. J."

Actor In the same packet is a simple document declaring that Nathaniel
    Pierston, infant son of Jennet Humfrye, is become by adoption the child
    of Morgan Thomas Drablow of Eel Marsh House, Crythin Gifford, and
    of his wife, Alice.

Silence. Then Kipps suddenly swings round as if the dog is startled

Kipps What is it, Spider?

*Silence. Then the rhythmic bump, bump, pause, bump, bump, pause. Kipps
stands. He hesitates, then moves purposefully forwards. At once, from
outside, comes the sound of a pony and trap*

   Stay with me, Spider, stay with me! (*He takes up the torch and moves
   outside*)

*The Lights fade and the only light is from Kipps's torch as the noise of the
pony's hooves gets louder and louder as if coming right up to the house.
Just as it seems the vehicle must come into our sight, it veers off the
causeway and we hear, as before, the sounds of it submerging. The child's
cry rises to a scream of terror, which is then choked and drowned*

Silence

*From the interior of the house, now distantly, we hear again the rhythmic
bump, bump, pause*

*Kipps moves inside. A light illuminates the door, and as we look, we see
it slowly open. The light is outside the door, but not inside. Kipps
approaches in fear and caution, then shines his torch inside. He walks
through. The only light comes from this torch, and we see by it that the
rocking chair is in motion—rocking backwards and forwards apparently
of its own volition—and it is this that we have heard, echoing on the floor
boards. As he shines his torch on it, it rocks less and less until it stops*

   But no-one had been there! No-one! There was no way out of the room
   except by the door I had come through, and no-one had passed me!

Pause

During the following, Kipps moves about the room, picking up occasional objects as they are mentioned

Actor It is a child's nursery. A bed in one corner, made up and all complete with pillows, sheets and counterpane, beside it, on the table, a tiny wooden horse and a nightlight. In the chest of drawers are clothes, underclothes, day clothes, formal clothes, play clothes, clothes for a small boy of six or seven. Beautiful, well-made clothes in the style of sixty years or more ago. And toys, most neatly and meticulously ordered and cared for. Lead soldiers, arranged in regiments. A farm, set out with barns and fences. A model ship, complete with masts and sails of linen. A whip. A spinning top. Ludo. Halma. Draughts and chess. A monkey made of leather. A cat of wool. A furry bear. A bald doll with a china head and a sailor suit. Pens and brushes, inks and dice, a miniature trumpet, a painted musical box from Switzerland, and a black doll with raggedy arms and legs.

Kipps (*holding, with tenderness, an object we can believe is this black doll*) They must have been here half a century, yet they might have been played with this afternoon. There was nothing here to frighten or harm me, there was only emptiness, a curious air of sadness, of something lost, missing, so that I myself felt a desolation, a grief in my own heart. How can I explain? I cannot. But I remember it as I felt it.

At length, he comes back out through the door, finds a chair, and sits. As he does, the wind begins to rise. Within a short time it is roaring around the house. Then, from the darkness outside, comes the child's cry of desperation and anguish. Kipps switches on the lights as:

The Woman in Black leaves the stage — momentarily glimpsed

Kipps swings round in horror. As he does so, a huge blast of wind hits the house and the Lights go out. Kipps begins to grope around in panic

The torch — God help me — the torch, Spider. Where is it, girl? (*He finds it*) Thank God, thank ——

He trips, the torch falls and goes out. He finds it again but it is broken. Then, in total darkness, he gropes his way back to the nursery, half panting, half sobbing — the wind howling as he goes, until he finds the nightlight and succeeds in lighting it. The wind continues to roar about the house. Kipps retraces his steps, out of the room, through the house, with only the candle for light. He sits, his head in his hands, the candle by him

Let it be morning ... let it be light.

From outside, comes the sound of someone whistling — as one whistles a dog

Spider ...?

Kipps stands, and taking his candle, moves to open the outside door

Who is it, Spider — who is it, girl?
Actor Before he can restrain her she is off, as though after a hare. Running low and fast, out of the house and away across the marshes.
Kipps Spider! Come back, Spider! Come back!

Again the whistle. As Kipps moves violently forward, the candle is extinguished

Spider!

Imperceptibly, the dawn begins to break. Throughout the following, the wind rages, and Kipps moves to the forestage and steps

During the next sequence, the Woman in Black is engaged in rendering the nursery area an utter shambles. She is outside the light, yet we see her as a crow-like silhouette, violently flapping in the dark

Actor He stands amazed and bewildered, as Spider's small form recedes into the great, open expanse. Then he runs as he has never run before!

We hear Kipps's footsteps, pounding furiously

She is floundering in mud. Fighting to retain her balance from the pull beneath her feet. She is yelping loudly ——
Kipps Spider!
Actor Still just visible ——

Kipps I'm coming, Spider — hold on, girl ——

Again the whistle

> Then he too begins to feel the stickiness and unsteadiness of the ground
> as it becomes boggier.

Kipps Stay still, Spider — still as you can ——

Actor He is obliged to wade rather than walk.

Kipps Have courage — I'm coming ——

Actor The little dog can scarcely hold up — her legs and half her body
have disappeared beneath the whirling, sucking bog, and her pointed
head is held up in the air as she struggles and yelps.

Kipps Good girl — good girl ...

Again the whistle

> Keep trying, Spider — keep trying, good girl ... (*He lies down, and fully*
> *extended, reaches for the dog*)

Actor He grabs her neck, just as the last of her body sinks. He hauls and
strains with a strength born of terror, he feels his grip on the slippery wet
fur give, the dog begins to slide away, then with a huge last effort he
drags his body backwards on to firmer ground.

The dog is suddenly released from the mud. Kipps rolls back, exhausted

Kipps (*relieved and tearful*) Oh, Spider, Spider — thank God, thank
God ...

He lies a while in silence, then looks up

> *The Woman in Black stands, looking directly down at him*

He stares at her, then screams. Then from the back of the theatre comes
the sound of a pony and trap. Black-out

> *The Woman in Black exits*

In the Black-out, the Actor, as Samuel Daily, moves to Kipps and shines
a torch into Kipps's eyes, attempting to rouse him

Sam Daily Mr Kipps — Arthur ...

The Lights fade up slowly as Kipps comes round

Kipps (*feverishly*) The trap — the pony and trap ——
Sam Daily Just over there. I still like to make use of it now and again —
  it's a pleasant way to travel. (*Pause*) What did you think?
Kipps I heard others — another ...
Sam Daily Oh, yes. (*Pause*) Not Keckwick?
Kipps No.
Sam Daily No. (*Pause*) You take care now.
Kipps I'm better. I'm all right.

Pause

Sam Daily I had you on my mind. I wasn't happy. It began to unsettle me.
Kipps Isn't it quite early in the morning ...? I've become confused.
Sam Daily Early enough. I kept waking. As I said, I had you on my mind.
Kipps How strange.
Sam Daily Was it? Not as it seems to me. Not strange at all.
Kipps No.
Sam Daily A good job I came when I did.
Kipps Yes, indeed, I'm very grateful. I'm extremely glad to see you, Mr
  Daily.
Sam Daily People have drowned on that marsh before now.
Kipps Yes. Yes, I know that now. I felt that I was being pulled under and
  the dog with me. (*He starts up*) Spider ...
Sam Daily She's here. She'll do. Now when you've come to a bit more,
  you'd better get whatever you need and we'll be off.
Kipps Off?
Sam Daily Ay. I came to see how you were faring in this Godforsaken
  place. I have seen. You had better come back home with me and recover
  yourself.
Kipps (*after a pause*) Thank you. I shall gather my things. I shan't be long.

Kipps moves through the house. He finds, in particular, the small packet
of letters and documents he had been reading. These he picks up, together
with his overnight bag. He is about to go downstairs when he sees the door
to the nursery ajar. He moves to look in, striking a match by which to see.

The full extent of the devastation is revealed

Dear God in Heaven!

He picks up various broken objects as he looks around him, and puts them down again. Then, in sudden fear, runs from the room to join Daily

The Actor, as Daily, moves the skip to represent the trap once more, as Kipps comes up to him

Sam Daily Come on then, Arthur, in you get. We'll be home in no time.

Kipps, as he climbs up, stumbles. Daily helps him, then climbs up himself

Spider — come on now, up! Good lass.

The pony and trap drives off. As it goes into the fading light, Kipps looks back to the house. There is no-one there

Black-out

Samuel Daily exits

The Lights return. Kipps draws up a chair to the side of the skip — using it as a desk. He opens the packet of letters and takes them out

Kipps (*reading a death certificate*) Nathaniel Drablow, age six years; cause of death: drowning. (*Reading another*) Rose Judd, nursemaid; cause of death: drowning. (*Reading another*) Jennet Eliza Humfrye, spinster, age thirty-six; cause of death: heart failure.

Silence

Samuel Daily enters with a decanter of whisky and two glasses. He sets them on the skip and sits opposite

Sam Daily (*pouring a glass for Kipps*) Well, you have come a long way since the night I met you on the late train.
Kipps It feels like a hundred years ago.

Sam Daily You've gone through some rough seas.

Pause. They drink

Kipps Do you suppose that poor Mrs Drablow was haunted night and day
by the ghost of that woman in black?
Sam Daily Jennet Humfrye. She was her sister.

Silence

Kipps Do you suppose she had to endure those dreadful noises out there?
If such was the case, I wonder how she could have endured it without
going out of her mind?
Sam Daily Perhaps she did not.
Kipps Perhaps. (*Pause*) Was there something I still did not see? If I had
stayed there any longer would I have encountered yet more horrors?
Sam Daily That I cannot tell.
Kipps But you could tell me something.

Daily shifts uneasily

Come, we're a good way from the place and my nerves are quite steady
again. (*A pause, then, to give the lie to this last statement, an edge of
hysteria comes in his voice*) I must know! It can't hurt me now!
Sam Daily Not you. No, not you maybe.
Kipps What are you holding back?
Sam Daily You, Arthur, will be away from here tomorrow or the next day.
You, if you are lucky, will neither hear nor see nor know of anything to
do with that damned place again. The rest of us have to stay. We've to
live with it.
Kipps With what? Stories — rumours? With the sight of that woman in
black from time to time? With what?
Sam Daily With whatever will surely follow. Sometime or other. Crythin
Gifford has lived with that for fifty years. It's changed people. They
don't speak of it, you found that out. Those who have suffered worst say
least — Jerome, Keckwick. (*He pauses and helps himself to more
whisky*) Jennet Humfrye gave up her child, the boy, to her sister, Alice
Drablow, and Alice's husband, because she'd no choice. At first she
stayed away — hundred of miles away. But, in the end, the pain of being

parted from him, instead of easing, grew worse and she returned to
Crythin. She got rooms in the town. She'd no money. She took in
sewing, she acted as a companion to a lady. At first, apparently, Alice
Drablow would not let her see the boy at all. But Jennet was so distressed
that she threatened violence and in the end the sister relented — just so
far. Jennet could visit very occasionally, but never see the boy alone nor
ever disclose who she was or that she had any relationship to him. No-
one ever foresaw that he'd turn out to look so like her, nor that the natural
affinity between them would grow out. He became more and more
attached to her, and as he did so, he began to be colder to Alice Drablow.
Jennet planned to take him away, that much I do know. Before she could
do so the accident happened, just as you heard. The boy ... the
nursemaid, the pony, trap and its driver, Keckwick ——

Kipps Keckwick!

Sam Daily Keckwick's father. And there was the boy's little dog, too.
That's a treacherous place, as you've found out to your cost. The sea fret
sweeps over the marshes suddenly, the quicksands are hidden.

Kipps So they all drowned.

Sam Daily And Jennet was at the house, watching at an upper window,
waiting for them to return. The bodies were recovered but they left the
pony and trap, it was held too fast by the mud. From that day Jennet
Humfrye began to go mad.

Kipps Was there any wonder?

Sam Daily No. Mad with grief and mad with anger and a desire for
revenge. She blamed her sister who had let them go out that day, though
it was no-one's fault, the mist comes without warning.

Kipps Out of a clear sky.

Sam Daily Whether because of her loss and her madness or what, she also
contracted a disease which caused her to begin to waste away. The flesh
shrank from her bones, the colour was drained from her, she looked like
a walking skeleton — a living spectre. Children were terrified of her.
She died eventually. She died in hatred and misery. And as soon as ever
she died, the hauntings began.

Kipps Well, Mrs Drablow is dead. There, surely, the whole matter will
rest.

Sam Daily And whenever she has been seen, in the graveyard, on the
marsh, in the streets of the town, however briefly, and whoever by, there
has been one sure and certain result.

Kipps (*whispering*) Yes?

Sam Daily In some violent or dreadful circumstance, a child has died.

Kipps What — you mean by accident?

Sam Daily Generally an accident. But once or twice it has been after an illness, which has struck them down within a day or night or less.

Kipps You mean any child? A child of the town?

Sam Daily Any child. Jerome's child.

Kipps But surely ... well ... children sometimes do die.

Sam Daily They do.

Kipps And is there anything more than chance to connect these deaths with the appearance of that woman?

Sam Daily You may find it hard to believe. You may doubt it.

Kipps Well, I ——

Sam Daily We know.

Silence

Kipps I do not doubt, Mr Daily.

The Lights begin to pulse and blur as the last verbal exchange is repeated as a voice-over, echoing in Kipps's mind

Sam Daily's voice You may find it hard to believe. You may doubt it.

Kipps's voice Well, I ——

Sam Daily's voice We know.

Sam Daily Arthur ——

Kipps's voice I do not doubt, Mr Daily.

Sam Daily Arthur ——

Sam Daily's voice We know.

Kipps's voice I do not doubt, Mr Daily.

Sam Daily's voice We know.

Sam Daily Arthur ——

As Kipps falls, Sam Daily catches him, lays him gently down and covers him with the blanket, which is the overture to Kipp's delirium. In the sequence, snatches of dialogue return to haunt him, in the form of voice-overs. The words are distorted, blurred, accompanied by sounds of the pony and trap

There are momentary glimpses of the Woman in Black

It's a whirling nightmare, in which, at its climax, Kipps screams

Voices And now it's your turn ... I have no story ... A foul day, Tomes ...
Dead, don't y'know?... Have you ever heard of the Nine Lives Causeway? ... Stella. Scribble a note to ... Dead, don't y'know?... One minute
it's as clear as a June day, the next ... Stella ... The Drablow papers, sir
.. She could hardly do otherwise, living there ... Is there a family
grave?... Behold. I show you a mystery ... I did not see a young woman
... Stella ... Dead, don't y'know ... Keckwick will come for you ... How
did you get out!... I wouldn't have left you over the night ... Stella ... You
will find no-one suitable ... a woman ... so I said once ... a woman ... not
another living soul ... a woman in black ... Such things one must face ...
a woman ... whistling ... a woman in black with a wasted face ... you are
whistling in the dark ... you shouldn't go there .... Drablow!... alone, you
shouldn't go there ... dead, don't y'know ... Stella!... alone ... But he is
mine ... I ... Spider!... I think my heart will break ... Spider!... Come
back!... he can never be yours!... a child ... Stella!... never ... Stella!... in
hatred .... never .... a child ... he can never, never, never be yours!
Kipps (*screaming*) Stella!

*A substantial Black-out. Then there is birdsong which gives way to the
sound of a pleasure park — music, laughter, many voices — as a spot
comes up on Kipps at the side of the stage*

There is only the last thing left to tell. Within a few weeks Stella and I
were married, and a little over a year later, Stella gave birth to our child,
a son, whom we called Joseph Arthur Samuel, and Mr Samuel Daily was
his godfather. I never thought of the past, I was filled with joy and
contentment in my life. I was in a particularly peaceful, happy frame of
mind one Sunday afternoon the following summer. We had gone to a
large park, ten miles or so outside London. There was a festive, holiday
air about the place, a lake, a bandstand, stalls selling ices and fruit.
Families strolled in the sunshine, children tumbled on the grass. Stella
and I walked happily, with young Joseph taking a few unsteady steps,
holding on to our hands. One of the attractions on offer was a pony and
trap on which rides could be taken, and little Joseph gestured to it
excitedly.

*We hear the pony and trap begin to draw away. There is a babble of
conversation, and the strains of the band playing a jolly tune*

So, because there was only room for two, Stella took Joseph and I stood, watching them bowl merrily down the ride. For a while they went out of sight away round a bend, and I began to look idly about me, at the other enjoyers of the afternoon. And then, quite suddenly, I saw her.

A spot illuminates the Woman in Black

The pony and trap draws nearer, we hear a child's laughter, the sound of the band, voices. The spot leaves Kipps and we watch the Woman in Black staring as if the trap is bearing towards her. Then, on a sudden movement from her, we hear the neighing of a startled horse, shouts from the driver, shouts of terror from the child, and then a horrifying crash

There is a second while the Woman in Black remains in the spot. Then she is gone

(*As the spot slowly finds him*) Our baby son had been thrown clear, clear against another tree. He lay crumpled on the grass below it, dead. And ten months later, Stella too, died from her terrible injuries. (*Pause*) I had seen the ghost of Jennet Humfrye, and she had had her revenge. You asked for my story, I have told it. Enough.

Silence. Then Kipps crosses and switches on the workers. The Actor comes to him, and in silence shakes his hand

Actor (*at length*) Thank you.

Kipps Thank *you*. (*Pause*) And is it done, d'you think? Will it now be laid to rest?

Actor I pray it will. I thank you for your trouble — your enthusiasm — and your effort. Your emotion just now — it was as if I watched myself.

Kipps I imagined my own child ...

Actor (*quickly*) Yes. (*He shudders involuntarily*) I pray that when we show it to our audience, at last it will be done with.

Kipps Who is she?

Actor I beg your pardon?

Kipps Your surprise. She is remarkable. Where did you find her?

Actor I'm afraid I don't understand.

Kipps Your surprise, Mr Kipps — the surprise you found for me.

Pause

Actor (*puzzled*) My surprise was that I'd learnt my words.

Kipps Yes, yes, you learnt them expertly, but the woman you found —
the actress. The woman in black. (*Pause*) Who was she? (*Pause*) You
organized it as a complete surprise — you had her come here and go
through her part and ... a young woman. With a wasted face — she ...

Silence. The Actor is staring at him in horror

Actor A *young* woman?

Kipps Is there anything the matter? You look unwell.

Pause

Actor (*at length*) I did not see a young woman.

*As the Lights fade, we hear again the rhythmic bump, bump, pause ...
bump, bump, pause ...*

Black-out

CURTAIN

FURNITURE AND PROPERTY LIST

ACT I

On stage: *Area downstage*
2 chairs
High stool
Armchair
Large skip. *In it:* bottle of brandy, bundles of documents
Blanket
Ledger
Various boxes
Thick brown envelope marked "Drablow" for **Tomes**
Travelling bag and newspaper for **Kipps**
Notepaper for **Kipps**
Riding whip for **Keckwick**

Area upstage
Rocking chair
Small bed with bedclothes
Chest of drawers with child's clothes
Various toys
Bedside table. *On it:* nightlight
(All items covered with cloths)

Off stage: Briefcase (**Kipps**)

Personal: **Actor:** manuscript, will and spectacles (as **Bentley**), wallet
         containing cards (as **Sam Daily**)
      Kipps: manuscript pages, pen

ACT II

On stage: As before

Set: *Area downstage*
Torch (practical) for **Kipps**
Torch (practical) for **Sam Daily**

Strike: *During Black-out on page 38*
                 All cloths from items in upstage area

Off stage: Decanter of whisky and 2 glasses (**Sam Daily**)

Personal: **Kipps:** box of matches

LIGHTING PLOT

Practical fittings required: nil
Various interior and exterior settings

ACT I

To open: House Lights on, bring up working lights on stage

Cue 1   **Actor:** "It *must* be *told.*"   (Page 4)
Black-out. When ready, bring up working lights as before

Cue 2   **Kipps** switches off the workers   (Page 6)
Reduce lighting to performance state

Cue 3   **Kipps:** "I pray for God's protection on us all."   (Page 7)
Black-out. When ready, bring up working lights on stage

Cue 4   **Kipps:** "Recorded sound!"   (Page 13)
Fade to black-out. When ready, bring up lighting on
     downstage area

Cue 5   As the train swells to a crescendo   (Page 16)
Fade to black-out. When ready, bring up lighting downstage

Cue 6   **Kipps's voice:** "... branded as a witch ..."   (Page 17)
Crossfade to worker state

Cue 7   **Kipps** moves to go   (Page 18)
Fade to black-out. When ready, bring up bright, crisp, winter
     daylight effect downstage

Cue 8   **Kipps:** "Ah yes, of course."   (Page 19)
Increase to sunshine effect

Cue 9   Market noises fade; footsteps echo   (Page 19)
Lighting dims slightly to give filtered effect through trees

Cue 10   **Jerome** carries on walking   (Page 20)
Crossfade to church interior effect, extending lighting to
     centre aisle

Cue 11	**Priest's voice:** "... your labour is not in vain in the Lord."(Page 21)	
	Crossfade to daylight effect as before	
Cue 12	**Kipps** clicks his fingers towards the back of the theatre	(Page 23)
	Crossfade to worker state	
Cue 13	**Kipps** signals to the back of the theatre	(Page 24)
	Crossfade to exterior daylight effect on skip	
Cue 14	**Kipps:** "... nine lives causeway."	(Page 25)
	Isolate **Kipps**	
Cue 15	**Kipps:** "... with a slate roof."	(Page 25)
	Bring up lights on stage	
Cue 16	**Keckwick** climbs on to the skip and flicks the whip	(Page 26)
	Concentrate lighting on **Keckwick**; *then gradually fade*	
Cue 17	The **Actor** climbs off the skip	(Page 26)
	Snap up broad daylight effect on downstage area and centre aisle	
Cue 18	**Kipps** scrambles through the gauze	(Page 26)
	Bring up lighting upstage	
Cue 19	**Kipps** moves back through the gauze	(Page 27)
	Fade lighting upstage	
Cue 20	**Actor:** "... the extremes of his emotions."	(Page 27)
	Dim lighting on stage area	
Cue 21	**Kipps** switches on a light	(Page 28)
	Increase lighting slightly	
Cue 22	**Kipps** switches off the lights	(Page 29)
	Snap off all lighting on stage area, leaving centre aisle lit; gradually begin to dim overall	
Cue 23	**Actor:** "Imagine him now ..."	(Page 29)
	Begin dimming gradually to virtual darkness	
Cue 24	**Kipps:** "No! No! No! *Keckwick!*"	(Page 30)
	Black-out. When ready, bring up dim interior lighting on downstage area	

Cue 25   **Keckwick** stands at the foot of the steps   (Page 30)
             Crossfade to moonlight effect on downstage area

ACT II

To open: Desk area lit

Cue 26   **Jerome:** "So I said — once."   (Page 34)
             Fade on **Jerome**

Cue 27   **Kipps:** "... my whole spirit, towards itself."   (Page 36)
             Crossfade to give house interior effect on downstage area

Cue 28   **Kipps:** "Spider! Spider.— rabbits!"   (Page 37)
             Bring up lighting on upstage area

Cue 29   **Actor:** "... the sky losing its light."   (Page 37)
             *Fade upstage lighting, reverting to house interior on
               downstage area*

Cue 30   **Kipps** sorts through the papers   (Page 37)
             *Fade to black-out. When ready, bring up house interior
               lighting as before*

Cue 31   **Kipps:** "Good-night now. Good-night."   (Page 38)
             Fade to black-out; then suddenly bring up shaft of moonlight

Cue 32   **Kipps** moves cautiously through the house   (Page 38)
             *Moonlight appears and disappears as if through many
               windows*

Cue 33   **Kipps** pushes against the door slightly with his shoulder (Page 38)
             Fade moonlight and begin gradual fade up on dawn effect

Cue 34   **Actor:** "He works through the day ..."   (Page 39)
             Crossfade to house interior effect on downstage area

Cue 35   **Kipps** takes up the torch and moves outside   (Page 40)
             Fade to black-out

Cue 36   **Kipps** moves inside   (Page 40)
             Bring up spot on closed door

Cue 37	**Kipps** switches on the lights *Bring up house interior effect on downstage area*	(Page 41)
Cue 38	Huge blast of wind *Black-out*	(Page 41)
Cue 39	**Kipps:** "Spider!" *Imperceptibly, fade up dawn effect on downstage area, gradually increasing*	(Page 42)
Cue 40	**Kipps** moves to the forestage *Silhouette effect on* **Woman in Black**	(Page 42)
Cue 41	Sound of pony and trap *Black-out*	(Page 43)
Cue 42	**Sam Daily:** "Mr Kipps — Arthur ..." *Slow fade up on downstage area*	(Page 44)
Cue 43	**Sam Daily:** "Good lass." *Gradual fade to black-out. When ready, bring up interior effect on downstage area*	(Page 45)
Cue 44	**Kipps:** "I do not doubt, Mr Daily." *Lighting begins to pulse and blur*	(Page 48)
Cue 45	**Kipps:** "Stella!" *Black-out. When ready, bring up spot on* **Kipps**	(Page 49)
Cue 46	**Kipps:** "And then, quite suddenly, I saw her." *Spot on* **Woman in Black**	(Page 50)
Cue 47	Sound effect of a child's laughter, etc. *Snap off spot on* **Kipps**	(Page 50)
Cue 48	The **Woman in Black** goes *Transfer spot slowly to* **Kipps**	(Page 50)
Cue 49	**Kipps** crosses and switches on the workers *Snap off spot, bring up worker state*	(Page 50)
Cue 50	**Actor:** "I did not see a young woman." *Fade to black-out*	(Page 51)

EFFECTS PLOT

ACT I

Cue 1   **Kipps** clicks his fingers to the back of the theatre   (Page 7)
London street sounds: cars, horses, street vendors' shouts, etc.

Cue 2   **Kipps** clicks his fingers again   (Page 8)
Street sounds fade, dissolving into sonorous ticking of long-case clock

Cue 3   **Actor:** "Remarkable."   (Page 8)
Clock fades out and street sounds return

Cue 4   **Kipps:** "I thank you!"   (Page 8)
Street sounds give way to sonorous clock ticking; continue

Cue 5   **Bentley:** "Children."   (Page 11)
Church bells toll in the distance; clock ticking continues

Cue 6   **Bentley** stands and moves away from the desk   (Page 12)
Fade clock ticking and church bells

Cue 7   When the Lights come up again downstage   (Page 13)
Sounds of steam trains and general railway station bustle

Cue 8   **Actor:** "... enclosed as some lamplit study."   (Page 13)
Fade station sounds; bring up moving steam train sound, then coming to a halt at station, etc. as in script pages 13-16

Cue 9   **Kipps** settles in an armchair   (Page 16)
Murmur of voices from public bar

Cue 10   **Kipps** resumes his letter   (Page 17)
Fade public bar voices, **Kipps's voice** *as script page 17*

Cue 11   The Lights come up   (Page 18)
Market place hubbub; continue

Cue 12   They step into the sunshine   (Page 19)
            Intensify market-place noises

Cue 13   **Kipps:** "... prevailing mood of the place." (Page 19)
            Market noises lull

Cue 14   **Kipps** smiles across at **Jerome**   (Page 19)
            Fade market noises; bring up footsteps echo effect

Cue 15   The Lights crossfade to church interior   (Page 20)
            Priest's voice, *interspersed with echoing tread, birdsong,*
                etc. as script pages 20-22

Cue 16   The Lights crossfade to a performance state   (Page 24)
            Sound of a pony and trap

Cue 17   The **Actor** sits facing out front   (Page 24)
            The pony draws to a halt

Cue 18   **Keckwick** clucks at the pony   (Page 25)
            The pony and trap set off; continue and intersperse with
                occasional, harsh , weird cries from birds

Cue 19   **Keckwick** reins in the pony   (Page 25)
            The pony draws to a halt

Cue 20   **Keckwick** flicks his whip   (Page 26)
            Pony hooves across the gravel; fading into the distance

Cue 21   The Lights reveal the shrouded furniture   (Page 26)
            Sudden, harsh bird cry; echoing and beating of wings

Cue 22   **Kipps:** "I did not believe in ghosts."   (Page 27)
            Sound of Kipps running: thud of footsteps and panting of
                his breath

Cue 23   Actor: "... the extremes of his emotions."   (Page 27)
            Door slam

Cue 24   **Kipps:** "I did not believe in ghosts."   (Page 28)
            Clock strikes deep in the house

Cue 25   **Kipps** locks up   (Page 29)
            Door slam

Cue 26   **Kipps:** "A nightmare walk, until ..."   (Page 29)
              Fade up sound of pony and trap and continue as
              described in script, page 30, together with marsh sound,
              horse whinnying in panic, terrified sobbing, etc.

Cue 27   Black-out. Pause   (Page 30)
              Door slam

Cue 28   **Keckwick** stands at the foot of the stairs   (Page 31)
              Doorbell

Cue 29   **Kipps** climbs up on to the skip   (Page 31)
              Pony and trap set off

ACT II

Cue 30   To open   (Page 32)
              Sound of busy market town

Cue 31   **Kipps** stands, crosses the stage   (Page 37)
              Door slam

Cue 32   **Actor:** "... the sky losing its light."   (Page 37)
              Door slam

Cue 33   **Kipps:** "What is it, Spider? What is it?" Pause   (Page 38)
              Distant, intermittent rhythmic bump. Cut after a while

Cue 34   **Kipps** moves away from his bed   (Page 38)
              Distant sound of intermittent rhythmic bump. Continue
              and increase in volume until **Kipps** *approaches the*
              closed door

Cue 35   **Kipps** stands as if paralysed   (Page 38)
              Barely audible, distant child's cry; gradually fade
              intermittent bump

Cue 36   **Actor:** "... never be parted."   (Page 39)
              Young Woman's voice *as script page 39*

Cue 37   **Kipps:** "What is it, Spider?"   (Page 40)
              Intermittent, rhythmic bump sound in distance as before

Cue 38	**Kipps** moves purposefully forwards *Sound of pony and trap as described in script pages 35-37, followed by a child's scream. Pause, then distant rhythmic bump sound*	(Page 40)
Cue 39	**Kipps** sits *Wind begins to rise, increasing in intensity; continue. Child's desperate cry from outside*	(Page 41)
Cue 40	**Kipps** swings round in horror *Huge blast of wind, continue wind howling effect*	(Page 41)
Cue 41	**Kipps**: "... let it be light." *Someone whistling outside*	(Page 42)
Cue 42	**Kipps**: "Come back!" *Whistle from outside*	(Page 42)
Cue 43	**Kipps**: "Spider!" *Wind rages*	(Page 42)
Cue 44	**Actor**: "... as he has never run before!" **Kipps's** *footsteps pounding furiously*	(Page 42)
Cue 45	**Kipps**: "— hold on, girl ——" *Whistle*	(Page 43)
Cue 46	**Kipps**: "Good girl — good girl ..." *Whistle*	(Page 43)
Cue 47	**Kipps** stares at the **Woman in Black** *Sound of pony and trap from back of theatre*	(Page 43)
Cue 48	Black-out *Cut wind howling*	(Page 43)
Cue 49	**Sam Daily**: "Good lass." *Pony and trap drives off*	(Page 45)
Cue 50	**Kipps**: "I do not doubt, Mr Daily." **Kipps's** *and* **Sam Daily's** *voices as script page 48*	(Page 48)
Cue 51	**Sam Daily** covers **Kipps** with the blanket *Distorted, blurred voices as script page 49, accompanied by sounds of the pony and trap*	(Page 49)

Cue 52   Black-out   (Page 49)
          Birdsong, giving way to pleasure park sounds, etc.,
              as described in script pages 49-50, culminating in
              horrifying crash

Cue 53   As the Lights fade   (Page 51)
          Rhythmic bump sound

MADE AND PRINTED IN GREAT BRITAIN BY
LATIMER TREND & COMPANY LTD PLYMOUTH

MADE IN ENGLAND